The Story of the Internet

STEPHEN BRYANT

Level 5

Consultant Editor: David Evans
Series Editors: Andy Hopkins and Jocelyn Potter

Pearson Education Limited
Edinburgh Gate, Harlow,
Essex CM20 2JE, England
and Associated Companies throughout the world.

ISBN 0 582 43047 X

First published 2000

5 7 9 10 8 6

Typeset by Ferdinand Pageworks, London
Set in 11/14pt Bembo
Printed in China
SWTC/05

Published by Pearson Education Limited in association with
Penguin Books Ltd, both companies being subsidiaries of Pearson Plc

For a complete list of titles available in the Penguin Readers series please write to your local
Pearson Education office or contact: Penguin Readers Marketing Department,
Pearson Education, Edinburgh Gate, Harlow, Essex, CM20 2JE.

Contents

Business Wordlist

accountant	a person who reports the finances of a company
bid	an offer to do work, provide a service or pay a particular price for something
branch	part of a large organization, often a shop or an office
capital	money that helps to build a new business
consultant	a person who gives business advice
corporation	a big company
to expand	to increase or grow
expert	a person with special knowledge of a subject
link	a connection or a relationship between people, organizations, ideas or things
loan	money that has been lent
negotiate	to try to come to an agreement with another person
network	a system that connects people, organizations or things together
objective	a business aim
partnership	a business that is owned by two or more people
project	a piece of work that needs knowledge, skill and planning
publish	to print something and offer it for sale to the public
sack	to tell someone to leave their job
share	a piece of paper that says you own a part of a company
stock exchange	a place where people buy and sell shares
trade	to buy and sell

Introduction

'This software's going to change everything. Soon everyone will be using it,' Marc Andreessen said to John Doerr. John often heard claims like this. His job was finding finance for new companies. So every day he met people who were confident that their ideas were going to change the world and make millions of dollars in the process. But Marc and his plan were different.

Marc was only twenty-three years old, but already he had a good reason to be confident. A few months before, he had written a program called Mosaic. Now two million people were using it.

At the time when Marc Andreessen said that his software was going to change everything, the Internet was just a hobby for most of the people who used it. People said that no one made money from the Internet. But before there were roads, people had said that you could not make money from cars. They had said that you could not sell telephones when there was no one to call.

In 1994, Marc Andreessen was one of the few people who saw the commercial possibilities of the Internet. His company, Netscape, allowed ordinary people to take advantage of a technology that, until then, had only been used by scientists and engineers.

The Internet began as a very small part of America's struggle with the Soviet Union in the Cold War. But it starts the twenty-first century as the technology that will change the lives of almost every person on the planet. This is its story.

Chapter 1   Sputnik

Until the evening of 4 October 1957, the US President, Dwight D. Eisenhower, was confident that he led the world's greatest nation. In the USA, the early 1950s are known as the Eisenhower years. Many Americans remember these years as a time of wealth and happiness. The USA was the richest nation in the world and it was growing richer all the time. Almost every American could hope to own a house and a car. As a general, Eisenhower had led US armed forces to victory in the Second World War and, until that evening in 1957, it seemed that no other nation could threaten the USA.

But then some news arrived that shook America's belief in itself: 'The Russians are in space! The Russians are in space!' Until this moment Americans believed that their nation was the most powerful on Earth. But now the Soviet Union had gone beyond the Earth.

Millions of radios all over the world could hear a new broadcast: 'Beep ... beep ... beep ...' This electronic noise was the sound of the satellite Sputnik 1, the first object placed in space by humans. It was a Russian achievement and it shocked Americans.

This was the time of the Cold War. The Soviet Union was America's great enemy, and soldiers from both sides stood ready to fight in almost every part of the world. The risk of real fighting – a 'hot' war – was always present. But the Cold War was not just about armies and weapons. It was also a war of technology and ideas. Each side presented its successes in science and technology as proof that its political system was better.

So when the Soviet Union sent its little silver satellite up into

1

the cold night sky of the Kazakh Republic, it was more than just an interesting scientific test. It was an act that showed the world that the Soviet Union was winning the war of ideas. Sputnik measured just fifty-eight centimetres across. But every ninety-six minutes it crossed the skies of the USA like a new moon – a Russian moon.

Americans were worried. If the Russians could put a satellite into space, what else could they do? Soon they might send platforms into space as well, and drop bombs from them, right into the heart of the nation. Newspapers were soon filled with wild stories about the new dangers in space. Many Americans believed them.

◆

'What are we going to do about this?' President Eisenhower asked his Secretary of Defense, Neil McElroy.

'There's no real reason to worry,' McElroy replied. 'Sputnik is not a danger for us. Our scientists are better than their scientists.'

'I know that,' said the President. 'That's not what I'm worried about. My problem is that I don't like surprises. I don't want to be surprised like this again. The nation doesn't want to be surprised like this again. In future we will make sure that we are ahead of the Russians in all important technologies.'

'What are you suggesting, Mr President?'

'We need a new department of government to direct our high-technology work. I want to be able to say to the American people, "Don't worry. The best scientists in the world are working for the US government and they're keeping us ahead of the Russians." And I want to stop the armed forces competing with each other, the way they do now. It's a waste of money and talent. I want a single organization to control all our high-technology efforts.'

'Yes, sir, Mr President,' said McElroy.

The Secretary of Defense did not know it, but as he turned and walked out of the famous Oval Office, he was taking the first steps on a road that led to the most important invention of the late twentieth century: the Internet.

Chapter 2 The First Computer Network

On 7 January 1958, President Eisenhower announced a new organization called ARPA that would control all of the government's high-technology work.

Soon ARPA was spending millions of dollars on research into new science and technology. In lonely laboratories deep in the deserts and mountains of the USA, brilliant men and women explored extraordinary new ideas. Scientists built bombs that could spread terrible diseases. Engineers made plans for wars in space. Psychologists tried to train people to communicate through the power of thought alone.

ARPA's earliest projects were aimed at winning the 'space race' that Sputnik had started. But these projects were soon placed under the control of a new organization, NASA. NASA captured America's imagination all through the 1960s, especially after President Kennedy announced his plan to land a man on the moon.

While NASA filled the news, ARPA was working quietly in an area that would eventually prove far more important than space travel: computing.

◆

In 1966, the man in charge of ARPA's computer projects was Bob Taylor. He began his career as a scientist working on brain research. But he was also interested in computing, even before computer science existed as a separate area of study. Computers were still a very new technology at this time. They were less common than Rolls-Royce cars – and more expensive. In the 1960s, a computer with the power of the machines that sit on desks today cost millions of dollars and was the size of an apartment. Most of these machines were owned by universities, the government or large companies. They were mainly used for mathematics.

But even at this time, Bob Taylor realized that computers were not just machines that could calculate. They were machines that could communicate as well.

ARPA was paying for computer projects at universities all over the USA. But Bob Taylor was not happy with the results. He went to see his boss, Charlie Herzfeld:

'Charlie, we've got a problem,' he said.

'What's that?' Herzfeld asked.

'We're throwing money away,' said Taylor. 'We're paying different people all over the USA to do exactly the same work.'

'What's wrong with them?' shouted Herzfeld, who had a strong Austrian accent and frightened many of the people who worked for him. 'Haven't they heard of the telephone? Don't they go to conferences? We pay for them to go to conferences. Why don't they just tell each other what they're doing?'

'No, Charlie, that's not the problem,' explained Taylor. 'Of course our people talk to each other. The trouble is that their computers don't.'

'Their computers don't talk? What do you mean?' asked Herzfeld.

'Well, look at my office. I've got connections there to all of our biggest computers. But if I want to communicate with the people at Santa Monica, I have to sit down at one machine. And if I want to talk to the computer at Berkeley, I have to get up from that machine and go over and sit at another one, using a completely different computer language. It's the same for all the other computers.'

'So what's the answer, then?' asked Herzfeld.

'I want to build a network of computers. I'd like to connect four of our biggest computers together. Then the scientists can share their research and we won't be paying for the same jobs again and again.'

Herzfeld looked at Taylor for a moment.

'Isn't that going to be difficult?' he asked.

'Oh, no,' said Taylor, sounding more confident than he felt. 'We already know how to do it.'

Herzfeld thought for a moment.

'Great idea, Bob,' he said. 'Start working on it. I'll give you a million dollars right now. Go.'

Taylor left Herzfeld's office and went back to his own room. 'A million dollars!' he said to himself. 'And that only took twenty minutes! Why didn't I ask for more?'

♦

When Bob Taylor had the money for a network, he began to hire people to build it. His first choice for a manager of the project was Larry Roberts.

Roberts was perfect for the job because he was an expert in both computers and communications. He had just succeeded in linking two computers on opposite coasts of the USA. Bob Taylor had paid for this work and now he wanted Larry Roberts to go to work at ARPA. The problem was that Roberts did not want to come. He was happy where he was – Lincoln Laboratory at the Massachusetts Institute of Technology (MIT).

Taylor went to see Charlie Herzfeld again: 'Isn't it true that ARPA is giving Lincoln at least 51 per cent of its money?'

'Yes, it is,' said Herzfeld.

'Would you speak to Larry's boss and make sure he remembers who pays his wages?'

So Charlie Herzfeld called Roberts's boss at Lincoln. 'We control more than half of your money,' said Herzfeld. 'So it would be good for Larry Roberts and good for Lincoln Laboratory if Roberts came to ARPA. Why don't you send him down here as fast as you can?'

The boss of Lincoln Laboratory quickly called Larry Roberts into his office.

'It would probably be a good thing for all of us if you would take this job. They won't accept "no" for an answer.'

Two weeks later Larry Roberts was at ARPA.

◆

Bob Taylor gave Larry Roberts the job of finding computers for the new network. ARPA wanted to use some of the computers that it paid for at universities around the USA. But the people who controlled these machines were not enthusiastic.

'We've got our own work to do,' they said. 'Computer time is too valuable to waste on crazy ideas.'

Others were more worried about security:

'The information on these computers is secret,' they told Larry Roberts. 'If my computer starts talking to your computer tomorrow, it'll be talking to the whole of the Soviet Union by the end of the week!'

None of the scientists seemed to trust anyone who was not at their own university. 'I don't want any fools from University X to touch my million-dollar computer,' they said. But all of them seemed quite happy to think that they might get their hands on other people's computers.

Larry Roberts went for help to Bob Taylor. Taylor simply used the same methods of persuasion that he had used to get Larry Roberts to ARPA. He phoned each of the universities and said, 'Who pays for your computer?'

'You do,' they replied.

'Then you're going to join this network,' said Bob Taylor.

So ARPA got the computers for its network, which Taylor had decided to call the ARPAnet. But it was 1966 and no one in the world really knew how to build a network.

◆

Larry Roberts began to make plans. He had the money and he had permission to join together four big computers. But the really important questions about the design of the network had no answers yet.

Bob Taylor held a conference for ARPA's computer researchers at Ann Arbor, Michigan, in early 1967. This was Larry Roberts's chance to describe his plans and hear the opinions of the best computer scientists in the USA. At first they were not enthusiastic.

Roberts said that he planned to join the computers together directly, with telephone lines. This meant that the 'host' computers would do two jobs: the work they already did, and the extra work of controlling the new network. Most of the audience hated this idea.

'Our computers have too much work already. They can't do another job,' they said. 'Anyway, this network won't work. Every computer in the system will need to understand how to talk to every other computer. There are just too many different types of computer and they all use different languages.'

This was a very good point, and Larry Roberts did not have an answer to it. Even if you could link two computers together on a phone line, it would be very hard for them to understand each other. It would be like French and Indian people trying to communicate in Swahili.

Just before the meeting ended, someone handed a note to Larry Roberts. 'You've got the network inside out,' it said.

The note was written by Wes Clark. He was one of the least enthusiastic members of Larry Roberts's audience. He was bored by the meeting and he had already told Roberts that he did not want to be part of the network. He was working on computers for individual users and he did not want to share them. Maybe this was why he saw a way to build a network that did not force the host computers to do more work.

After the conference was over, Larry Roberts found Wes Clark and asked him, 'What did you mean when you said "You've got the network inside out"?'

'I've got a plane to catch,' said Clark. 'Can we talk in the taxi?'

So Wes Clark and Larry Roberts continued their discussion on the way to the airport. Clark described his idea:

'Forget about sending a message from one computer to another directly. It'll never work. The host computers have got enough to do, already. Right?'

'Well, yes,' Roberts agreed. 'But we need them to do this networking for us. It will help everyone in the end.'

'Yes, yes, I know all that,' said Clark. 'But you don't need to make them do the extra work of translating between all the different computer languages as well.'

'But how can we avoid it?' Roberts asked.

'Why don't you design a system that uses other computers as translators? Then messages will always go through one of these translators before they go on to their destination.'

'How would that work?'

'You can leave the hosts as they are if you put a smaller computer between each of them and the phone lines. The small computers will all speak the same language. But each small computer only needs to learn just one new language, to speak to its host computer. And the little computers will run the network. They'll do all the work of checking the messages and sending them on, not the hosts. Leave the hosts as they are, build an inner network of small computers, and everything will be fine. It's obvious.'

'That's brilliant,' said Larry Roberts. He climbed out of the taxi with the seed of a new plan for the network growing in his mind.

Wes Clark's idea solved several problems. Obviously it meant less work for the host computers – and for the people who controlled them. It also meant that each host computer would only have to learn one new language, to speak to the smaller computers. And it gave ARPA better control of the whole network.

When Larry Roberts got back to Washington, he wrote a new plan for the ARPAnet, including Wes Clark's ideas. He called the new, smaller computers 'IMPs'. These IMPs would be the interface between the different host computers. In other words, they would allow two systems to meet and talk to each other.

The design of the ARPAnet was becoming clearer. But Larry Roberts still didn't know exactly how the IMPs should speak to each other.

♦

Roberts explained his latest ideas at another conference. This meeting was held at Gatlinburg, Tennessee, at the end of 1967. Roberts talked about the ARPAnet, the host computers, and the inner network of IMPs that would help the hosts to communicate. But he did not say much about how this communication would work. That was still not clear.

At the same meeting there was another talk by Roger Scantlebury, from the National Physical Laboratory in England. He spoke about how to build a 'packet-switched' network. To Larry Roberts, packet switching sounded perfect for the ARPAnet.

Packet switching is a very efficient way to send data electronically. Each message is broken down into pieces or 'packets'. The packets are then sent out into the communications network. There is no need for the packets to travel together or in any particular order. Each packet is free to find the best route to its destination. When all the packets have arrived, they are put back together again to form the original message.

There is nearly always more than one route to any destination through a network. If there are ten routes from A to B, it will be quicker to break a message into ten parts and send them all at the same time than to send the whole message along a single path.

Packet switching also takes advantage of the fact that the data used by nearly all computers is 'digital'. This means that the original information – sounds or pictures, for example – is translated into a system of numbers. Digital information is very easy to copy. It can easily be broken down into packets and put back together again without losing any data.

Vint Cerf is an engineer who has written some of the most important software for today's Internet. He said that digital packets are just like postcards:

'The best way to describe packet-switching technology is to remind you that packets are just like postcards. They've got "to" and "from" addresses on them and they've got a limited amount of content. And, like a postcard, you put them in the post box. If you put two in, you do not know what order they're going to come out in. They might not even come out on the same day. They do not necessarily follow the same paths to get to the destination. The only difference is that an electronic packet goes about a hundred million times faster than a postcard.'

◆

Now Larry Roberts had plans for the hardware and the software of the ARPAnet. The next question was, who could build it?

This was exactly what Larry Roberts asked Wes Clark when Clark gave him the idea for a network of IMPs.

'There's only one person in America who can build your network,' replied Wes Clark. 'Frank Heart.'

Larry Roberts knew Frank Heart. They had worked together at Lincoln Laboratory. Heart was an expert in 'real-time systems' – systems that work so quickly that human beings do not notice any delay at all. The ARPAnet did not need to be so fast. But to make packet switching work, lots of very complicated problems of timing would have to be solved. Frank Heart's skills seemed to make him the best man for the job. He was also known as someone who always finished what he started.

But Larry Roberts could not simply hire him. Contracts like the ARPAnet were supposed to be offered to many competitors so the government got the best deal. Roberts had to ask for bids from the best companies in the computer and communications industries. In August 1968, he wrote a plan and sent it to 140 technology companies.

'It can't be done,' replied most of them. The biggest names in the computer business at the time were sure that the network could not be built. Both IBM (International Business Machines) and Control Data Corporation said the job was impossible. They said no one could build the network for an acceptable price because the IMPs would have to be enormously expensive mainframe computers.

The telephone companies were even more negative. AT&T

controlled long-distance phone calls in the USA. 'You'll never make packet switching work,' it said.

The telephone companies had never been helpful to computer scientists:

'Please give us good data communications,' the scientists asked.

'We have phone lines everywhere. Use the telephone network,' said the telephone companies.

'But you don't understand,' said the scientists. 'It takes twenty-five seconds to arrange a call, you charge us for at least three minutes, and we only want to send less than a second of data.'

'Go away,' the telephone companies replied. 'We earn tiny sums from data compared to the money that we make from voice traffic.'

So the computer scientists went away – and they created the Internet.

One of the companies that bid to build the ARPAnet was Bolt, Beranek & Newman (BBN) of Cambridge, Massachusetts. BBN was the place where Frank Heart worked, and half the staff had already worked with Larry Roberts at Lincoln Laboratory.

Frank Heart gave ARPA's plan to his best programmer, Severo Ornstein. Heart said, 'Why don't you take this home and have a look at it and see what you think?'

Ornstein came back the next day and said, 'Well, sure, we could build that if you wanted to. But I can't see why anyone would want it.'

Ornstein did see a problem, though:

'BBN's a small company, so we'll have to put in a very, very good bid to win the contract.'

'Of course,' said Frank Heart. 'But what's the problem? We *are* very, very good, aren't we?'

'Yes,' Ornstein agreed. 'But isn't it a big problem that so many of us know Larry Roberts? He won't want to be seen passing out contracts to his old friends.'

Frank Heart did not agree.

'If the bid is good enough, we'll win,' he said.

♦

Frank Heart believed that a small company had an advantage in this situation. Unlike IBM or AT&T, BBN could move very quickly. For four weeks Heart and his team worked day and night. Later, some members of the team honestly believed that the work had taken six months, not one.

By the time they had finished, their plan was enormously detailed. They had worked out most of the design for the IMPs, using an existing computer from the Honeywell company. They described how the network could be made to work even under heavy loads. And they also discovered that they could make the system run ten times more quickly than ARPA was asking.

In the end BBN had only one serious competitor for the ARPAnet contract: the much bigger Raytheon Corporation. But the difference in size persuaded Larry Roberts to choose BBN.

'Why BBN and not Raytheon?' Bob Taylor asked him.

'BBN's bid is very good. It's as good as Raytheon's.'

'I agree,' said Bob Taylor. 'But why pick BBN and not Raytheon? Raytheon is bigger.'

'But that's just the problem,' Roberts replied. 'There are too many layers of managers at Raytheon. If something goes wrong, who do I call? At BBN everyone reports to Frank Heart. If there's a problem, I can just phone Frank and tell him to fix it.'

'BBN is a small company.'

'Don't worry. That will make them fast.'

Larry Roberts gave the contract to BBN. But the company would need to be fast. It only had nine months to complete the job.

♦

Frank Heart's team started work at the beginning of 1969, and the job had to be finished by 1 September. No one today knows why BBN was given so little time to build the ARPAnet.

'There probably isn't a reason,' Frank Heart said to his team. 'The government sometimes picks dates without thinking. This one is probably an artificial date picked by the government and picked by Larry Roberts. I don't know why they chose it. I can't see any reason why it has to be that particular day. But that's what it is. That is in the contract and so that's what we've got to do.'

They had several big jobs to do. The team had to make packet switching work in the real world. They had to turn an ordinary computer into an IMP. They had to write software to control the IMPs. And they had to work with the four host sites to make sure that the IMPs could communicate with their mainframes.

The biggest problem was the hardware.

'I'm worried that we won't get the hardware built in time,' said Frank Heart.

'We've done this kind of thing before,' said Severo Ornstein.

'Yes, but there's so much more to do this time,' said Heart. 'We have to design a computer. We have to get Honeywell to understand the design and build it. Then we need to test it.'

The IMPs were the heart of the network. Each IMP would stand between a host computer and the telephone system. It would have to translate messages from the host computer into packets for the network. When it received packets, it would have to know whether to build them into a message for its host or pass them on to another IMP. At any moment, all of the IMPs would have to know how the whole network was performing so they could send packets by the most efficient route.

Because the IMPs were so important, Frank Heart wanted to make sure that they would never break down. He also wanted them to be impossible to destroy. He imagined students at the host sites opening the IMPs and taking them apart. He tried very hard to make sure that this could not happen.

Frank Heart's worries about students were one of the main reasons that he decided to base the IMPs on Honeywell's DDP-516 computer. Honeywell sold this computer to the army. Frank Heart knew that the company had an interesting way of proving that the machine was strong enough to work in a war.

So, how do you prove that a computer will not break? To answer this question, Honeywell invited its customers into a large hall. There a DDP-516 was hanging from the ceiling.

'That's interesting,' the customer might say, 'but what does that tell us?'

'Look more closely,' the Honeywell people said. When the customer approached, he saw that the computer was actually working while it was swinging on a rope above the ground.

'That's very good.'

'Oh, no,' said the Honeywell people. 'Not really. But the next thing you'll see is certainly very, very good.'

At that moment a tall, strong man walked into the room carrying a large hammer. He swung the hammer, and with a great crash he hit the computer again . . . and again . . . and again.

When the computer had stopped swinging, the Honeywell people invited the customer to inspect it again.

'Check and see if it's working now,' they said. It always was. This was almost enough to calm Frank Heart's fears about students.

◆

The software for IMPs needed to be at least as good as the hardware. The software had to deliver whole messages to the correct destinations. For this, software had to be written that worked even if the hardware didn't – even if an evil student had managed to break one of Frank Heart's IMPs.

This is still the way the Internet works today: the software understands how to avoid broken hardware. If a packet does not reach its destination, the software knows. Then it sends that packet again, by a different route if necessary.

In the spring of 1969, both the software and the hardware were working in BBN's own building.

'Now we know the network will work,' said Severo Ornstein.

'Don't forget the messages are only travelling a few metres,' Frank Heart warned. 'That isn't a network. We still have to build a system that works over thousands of kilometres.'

'That's true,' Ornstein agreed. 'But we know that the principle is exactly the same if the wire is a metre long or a hundred kilometres long. The phone company says that the length of the wire doesn't matter. It's going to work!'

'I hope you're right,' said Heart.

◆

At the four host sites, the teams had even less time to build their parts of the network. And some of the team members had no experience of this kind of work. Vint Cerf was one of them. Every day he thought, 'When are the professional managers going to arrive? We're just graduate students.'

But there never were any professional managers. So Cerf and his friends just continued to do the work.

At each host site, the computer was a mainframe – a machine that was designed to behave like the only computer in the universe. In each case, this computer had to be connected to another computer – an IMP – for the first time. But each mainframe was different and needed a different set of connections.

'The question is, exactly how do they connect?' said Frank Heart. 'How do they connect electrically? How do they connect logically? How does the software connect? These are very difficult questions. And they have to be solved very, very, very quickly. Because we at BBN have to build special hardware into the Honeywell machine at our end of the connection, and all the host sites have to build special hardware for their mainframe computers and write special software to match our connection.'

ARPA was very clear about the network it wanted: one host computer connected to one IMP. But the host sites all had more than one big computer. Soon they were calling Frank Heart.

'Wait, wait!' they said. 'We've got more than one computer! We want to connect two or three computers to your IMP please!'

Heart was surprised. 'Why are you suddenly so keen on the network?' he asked. 'Only a few months ago, you were all saying "Leave us alone."'

'Well, yes, that's true,' said the people at the host sites. 'But now we can see how useful the network will be.'

'To share data with other sites?'

'Not really . . .'

'What, then?' Frank Heart wanted to know.

'Well, even here, just at this university, the computers can't talk to each other,' said the host sites. 'They're all made by different companies and they all use different software. But your IMP is designed to connect different machines together. If you let us connect all our computers to the IMP, then we'll be able to share data here much more easily.'

'So, you want me to build you a local network?'

'Yes, please.'

◆

On 16 July 1969, Neil Armstrong became the first man to walk on the moon. But at BBN there was not much time to watch the historic television broadcast. It was just six weeks before the first IMP was due to be delivered to the University of California at Los Angeles (UCLA). BBN heard that UCLA was not ready. UCLA believed that BBN was going to be late. Both teams were working twenty-four hours a day.

At BBN, Frank Heart was worried about transporting the IMP from Cambridge to Los Angeles. This was not simple in 1969, says Severo Ornstein: 'The ability to move a machine across the country was important. Today you carry machines around and you expect to switch them on and you just expect it all to work. But just a few years ago, computers were built into walls. And if you shook the room a little bit, it was days before you could make the machine work again.'

Frank Heart decided that the IMP should go to Los Angeles by air. Truett Thatch met it at Los Angeles airport and he was shocked to see that the box was the wrong way up: 'Somewhere along the way, the IMP had been turned over an odd number of times.' He made sure it was turned over again and went with it to the UCLA.

It was the Saturday before the Labor Day★ holiday and there were very few people at the university. But the whole UCLA network team was waiting outside the building. Vint Cerf had brought an expensive bottle of wine. It was immediately obvious that the box was too big to fit through the door. They had to take the IMP out of the box on the street.

Everyone at UCLA was surprised by the size and weight of the IMP. It was about the size of a fridge and it weighed nearly five hundred kilograms. The team had been thinking about almost nothing apart from the IMP for nine months. But it was

★ Labor Day: a national holiday to honour working people. In the USA, Labor Day is on the first Monday in September.

still a shock to actually see it. Steve Crocker was part of the UCLA team:

'It's a little like seeing your parents invite to dinner someone that you've never met. You don't pay much attention until you discover that they actually want you to marry this strange person.'

It took a few minutes to connect the IMP to the host computer. Then it was switched on. It began to run its software at exactly the same point where it had stopped back at BBN. Within an hour, the IMP and the host were exchanging information.

♦

The UCLA IMP and its host were the only machines on the network. Until another host computer was connected, the ARPAnet would not be a real network. One month later, on 1 October 1969, the second IMP was delivered to the Stanford Research Institute. The telephone lines were connected to both IMPs. Each IMP was connected to its host. Everything was turned on and the network was ready for its first message.

Vint Cerf was at UCLA. First, he tried to 'log on' to the host computer at Stanford – this means typing in some instructions that obtain permission to run programs on a computer. A computer scientist like Cerf usually logged on to computers many times a day. But no one had ever logged on to another computer over a network before. As he typed at the keyboard, he also had a voice connection to the other engineer at Stanford. Cerf typed an 'L' and spoke into the telephone:

'Did you get the "L"?' he asked.

'I got the "L",' said the other engineer.

Cerf typed an 'O'.

'What about that?' he asked. 'Did you get an "O"?'

'I got an "O".'

So Cerf typed a 'G', to complete the first word ever sent over a network. 'Did you get the "G"?' he asked.

'Uh, no. No "G" . . .'

The network had crashed.

'No problem!' said Vint Cerf. 'You got the "L" and the "O". Say them together, "L-O". Sounds like "Hello!", doesn't it?'

It only took a few more hours until the network worked properly. The first message was not important, but the event was. Despite all the theory and the tests which proved that the ARPAnet *should* work, the connection between UCLA and Stanford proved that the network *did* work. It was the first time that distant computers had ever talked to each other.

The ARPAnet was the first computer network. Soon it would become the heart of a network of networks – the Internet.

Chapter 3　　To the Internet

Two more hosts were planned in BBN's contract with ARPA. They were connected to the ARPAnet before the end of 1969, in Utah and Santa Barbara. Bob Taylor's idea of a network of four computers was a reality. Taylor left ARPA soon afterwards, but the network continued to grow.

Larry Roberts became the new boss of ARPA's computer department. He soon called Frank Heart at BBN:

'We'd like you to build more IMPs and connect more hosts to the network.'

'How many?' asked Frank Heart.

'As many as you can.'

'Really?'

'Yes,' replied Roberts. 'Every new site on the network is saving me money. Every time someone asks me for a new computer, I can say, "You should connect your existing machines to the network." In a few years, the network will pay for itself.'

The network was a great success for the hosts as well as ARPA. They did not lose any computer power, as they had feared; they could use computers at other sites, so they gained. And they could also work more efficiently. As Bob Taylor had planned, the universities could work together on projects instead of repeating each other's work.

♦

However, some effects of the network were not in the plan. For example, the telephone companies began to get calls from ARPAnet engineers:

'Your line from Santa Barbara to UCLA is in trouble,' the engineer might say.

'OK,' said the telephone company. 'Which end are you at?'

'Neither. I'm in Cambridge, Massachusetts.'

'Where?'

'Cambridge . . .'

'So how do you know about the lines in California?'

'I'm on the ARPAnet.'

'The what . . .?'

The IMPs were designed to make constant checks on the condition of the network. This meant that ARPA's engineers often knew more about the performance of the telephone system than the telephone companies that owned and operated it.

There were other new possibilities. With the network, BBN was able to send new software to the IMPs immediately, as soon as it was written. Before this, engineers had to fly from place to place with paper tapes in their bag. But now, if one of the IMPs had a problem, it was very often possible for BBN to fix it from the company's offices, many hundreds of kilometres away.

But the biggest surprise was that the network was soon being used mostly for something that was never part of Bob Taylor's plan – chat. Technically, the network worked exactly as it was designed to. Yet by 1973, three-quarters of all traffic on the ARPAnet was nothing to do with sharing data or programs or logging on to distant computers. It was electronic mail – e-mail.

Ray Tomlinson was the first person to send e-mail on the ARPAnet. He was an engineer at BBN and in 1972 he invented a simple program for sending files between computers. The big mainframe computers at the universities already had mail boxes for all the different people who used the machines. People could send messages to other people who used the same computer. But there was no e-mail between different computers.

Tomlinson's program changed this. The software opened a connection, sent a file to another computer and then sent a message back to say that the file had arrived safely at its destination. Since the mail boxes in computers are really just files, the next step was simple. Tomlinson changed his program so that it carried a mail message from one computer and added it to a mail-box file of another machine.

Since everyone on the ARPAnet already had mail boxes in their host machines, it was easy to begin sending mail to other hosts. But the speed with which e-mail spread was surprising. Almost as soon as it was introduced, it took over the network. Even today, there are more individual e-mail messages sent over the Internet than data of any other kind.

Ray Tomlinson has left his mark on every single one of the billions of e-mails that have been sent since 1972. He was the person who chose the '@' sign which means 'at' in e-mail addresses. Why '@'?

'Well, at that time no one had an "@" sign in their name,' says

Tomlinson. 'I'm not sure that that is still true, because there are a lot of strangely spelled names out there now.'

◆

By 1972, the ARPAnet included dozens of sites. But hardly anyone knew about the network. Larry Roberts decided that this must change. He asked Bob Kahn at BBN to organize a public show. Kahn picked the International Conference on Computer Communication as the place to show the network to the world. The conference was held at the Hilton Hotel in Washington at the end of October.

Larry Roberts contacted all of the people around the USA who were now using his system. Many of them agreed to take part in the show. It was a real test of the network. In one example, a computer in Washington contacted another machine right across the country at UCLA and told it to run a program. When it had finished, this program then called Washington with the results and printed them out on a printer that sat on a table right next to the first computer.

There were also programs that allowed people to play games over thousands of kilometres. And a group from MIT brought a clever machine that was like a mechanical spider. This machine could be controlled over the network and guided through a room full of furniture, although its owners were many kilometres away.

But not everything went smoothly. The team with the printer could not make it work, although the network said that all the data was moving between the sites just as it was supposed to. Then someone looked around and noticed that the mechanical spider was jumping about in a mad dance. The UCLA computer had been connected to the spider by mistake – the dance was the data that was intended for the printer!

However, most of the problems were small and most of the guests at the conference were amazed by the network. After this, the ARPAnet began to grow even more rapidly. But now it was not the world's only network of computers.

◆

After the ARPAnet had shown that a computer network could be built and that it could be useful, other networks began to appear. Universities, government departments and other organizations saw that networking could multiply the power of their computers – and the power of the people who used them. But these new networks created their own rules. A system that was best for the ARPAnet did not necessarily suit other organizations with different needs, different styles of work and different hardware.

So, once again, there were many different computer systems that could not talk to each other. Now, just a few years after the ARPAnet was invented, the appearance of new networks had once again created the problem that had caused Bob Taylor to imagine the world's first computer network.

By this time, Bob Kahn was in charge of the ARPAnet project. He was very familiar with the new problem because he had worked on some of the newer networks. They were all designed to deal with different circumstances. For example, the Alohanet network in Hawaii used radio waves to deal with the problem of communicating over mountains and between different islands. The network in the San Francisco area was not even fixed: it was on lorries which moved around from place to place. The Atlantic Packet Satellite Network used another system, sending messages up to satellites in space to communicate across half the world.

On one of his visits to San Francisco, Bob Kahn went to see Vint Cerf, who was now at Stanford:

'I need to find a way to connect these new networks,' said Kahn. 'They're not like the ARPAnet. They all use their own software and hardware. It's a mess.'

'They're not going to change over to the ARPAnet system now,' said Cerf. 'They've spent too much money. And the systems work.'

'I know, but I still need a way to join them together. It's worse than before the ARPAnet – at least then we didn't know what a network could do.'

'So what do you want to do?' Cerf asked.

'I don't know. How do we make a network of networks?'

'The IMPs were the answer for the ARPAnet.'

'But they were built to link together different computers, not different networks,' said Bob Kahn. 'All these new networks have got their own IMPs, completely different to ours.'

'I know. But couldn't you still put something like an IMP between the different networks?'

'What do you mean?'

'Well, you need a kind of gate to each network,' said Cerf. 'The networks would still be under the control of their own IMPs. But the gate would tell each network how to communicate with the others.'

'So the gate is like an IMP – a box that stands between the different systems?'

'Yes,' said Cerf. 'But instead of translating between different computer systems, the gate will translate between different networks and reduce the number of differences between them.'

'Will you work with me on it?'

Vint Cerf agreed to work with Bob Kahn, and they began to write software that allowed different networks to communicate. In the set of rules that they invented in 1973, they used the word 'Internet' for the first time. It meant 'a network of networks'.

The software wrapped the messages from each different network inside Internet 'envelopes'. Then the messages could leave their home network and travel from one gate to another. There they were taken from the envelopes and sent into the second network. The risk of losing messages between different networks is much higher than the risk of losing them between different computers. But Cerf and Kahn's rules are still the glue that holds the Internet together today, more than a quarter of a century after they wrote them.

Bob Kahn and Vint Cerf thought that demand for the Internet would grow. But they never imagined the size of the growth. The late 1970s and 1980s saw an explosion in the use of computers and networks. The fuel for this explosion was the arrival of the personal computer.

Chapter 4   The Personal Computer

One night in January 1975, Bill Gates was playing cards with some friends at Harvard University. He was nineteen years old and he was studying law, but his first love was computers. Suddenly his friend Paul Allen rushed into the room carrying a magazine.

'Bill, come on, you've got to see this!'

'I'm playing cards,' said Bill.

'Are you winning?'

'No, but . . .'

'Well this is our chance to win big. It's what we've been waiting for,' said Paul.

Bill left his game and looked at the magazine that Paul had brought. On the magazine's cover was a picture of a new computer called the Altair. Paul and Bill were both amazed and excited. The Altair was what they had both been dreaming of – the world's first personal computer.

Bill and Paul had both loved computers for many years, from the time when they were at school in Seattle. They had already started a company together which used computers to calculate the best routes for traffic on busy roads. But both of them saw that the Altair was their big chance.

For years, they had believed that there would soon be personal computers – small machines that anyone could buy and use. New chips were being produced that had much of the power of the older mainframes but were tiny and cheap. But the computer industry was only interested in making big, expensive machines for business. And in 1975, the computer industry was almost completely controlled by one company: IBM.

'It's easy to forget how powerful IBM was,' says Bill Gates today. 'When you talk to young people who've only come into the industry recently, there's no way you can get that into their heads.'

In 1975, IBM *was* the computer industry. It was the biggest company in the business, and it was bigger, richer and much more powerful than all other computer companies together. If IBM saw no future for personal computers, how could the Altair succeed?

But Bill Gates and Paul Allen believed there could be an enormous market for machines like the Altair – a market of people just like them. They were people who loved computers and who would give anything to have their own machine.

'Wow!' said Bill Gates as he read about the Altair. 'We knew that someone was going to do something with these new chips. But it's hard to believe it's actually happened.'

'We've got to do something about it.'

'They're going to need software, right?'

'Right.'

'Well let's get them on the phone and tell them what we can do.'

'OK,' said Paul. 'I'll make the call.'

The company that was making the Altair was called MITS, in Albuquerque, New Mexico – nearly 3,220 kilometres away from Harvard. The company was owned by a man named Ed Roberts. Paul phoned Ed.

'We've got a really good program and it's just for your machine,' he said. 'It's nearly finished and we'd like to come and show it to you.'

'Fine,' said Ed Roberts. 'I'll meet you at the airport.'

However, Bill and Paul had a big problem. They had not actually written the program that they had promised. So they sat down and worked as hard as they could. After several days and nights at their desks, they had nearly finished a program that would allow the BASIC computer language to be used on the Altair computer.

But the day before the trip to Albuquerque, Paul said, 'There's still a problem, Bill.'

'What? Everything looks fine to me.'

'No – not a problem with the program. We haven't got enough cash to fly all the way to New Mexico.'

'How much have we got?'

'Just enough for one ticket.'

'Well, why don't you get some sleep,' said Bill. 'I'll stay up and finish the program and you can fly down and show it to Ed Roberts.'

So Paul Allen flew down alone. When Ed Roberts met him at the airport in Albuquerque, Paul was surprised. He expected the boss of a new technology company to look rich and powerful. But Ed seemed like Paul himself, but older. He was an engineer dressed in jeans who drove an old van. And MITS's factory and office was a very ordinary building in a cheap area of the town. It looked like any small engineering factory on the edge of a city. But it was the birth place of the personal computer – the machine that would change the world more than anything since the invention of the motor car.

◆

Ed Roberts did not really want to be the father of the personal computer. He wanted to be a doctor. But he had always loved engineering and he read all the books he could find about making your own machines. After a period in the air force, engineering seemed the best way to make a living. But by 1975, Ed Roberts owed almost $400,000 and MITS was close to going out of business.

The company sold equipment to people whose hobby was electronics. With parts from MITS, these people could build their own electronic calculator for less than a hundred dollars. At this time a similar machine cost four times as much in a shop. But other, bigger companies quickly entered the market, charging even lower prices than MITS. Soon Ed Roberts needed $65,000 just to stay in business.

But he had an idea for a new product. He explained it on a cassette tape that he sent to his friend Eddie Currie. Ed and Eddie exchanged cassette tapes because they were speaking so often on the telephone that they could not afford the bills. One day Eddie received a tape on which Ed sounded even more excited than usual:

'I'm going to build a computer!' he said. 'Something anyone can buy. And there are people out there who will buy it. People like us, who want a computer more than anything else. All the computers in the world seem to be locked up in enormous organizations, guarded by priests in white coats. I can end all that! Everyone can have their own machine! They can do anything they want with it! It'll be wonderful! I'll make it so cheap that no one can afford not to buy it!'

Eddie Currie thought that this was just another of Ed's crazy ideas. A complete computer? Only IBM did that. In fact Ed Roberts had no idea how difficult the project was going to be. But he did have a brilliant starting point: the new 8080 chip from Intel. The chip was as powerful as the mainframes from a few years ago. And if he could only buy the chip cheaply enough, he was sure his plan would work.

He phoned Intel.

'How much do you want for the 8080?'

'They're worth $350 each.'

'That's too much,' said Ed. 'But I need a lot of chips. What would the price be for a big order?'

'Well, how many chips do you need?'

Eventually Ed Roberts got the price down to $75 per chip. But only if he bought a very large quantity of chips. Of course, this meant that he could only save his business if he sold lots of the computers that he was going to build with the chip. And he needed more money before he could start.

Ed went to his bank for a meeting late one night. He explained his plan to build and sell a personal computer. Finally he said, 'The question is, do I close down MITS or do you lend me $65,000?'

'How many machines will you sell in the first year?' asked the banker.

'Eight hundred,' said Ed.

'That sounds very optimistic.'

The bank manager was doubtful that Ed Roberts could sell very many personal computers. But he was persuaded by Ed's positive attitude, so Ed got his money and announced the Altair. And within a month he was getting 250 orders every day. It seemed there were lots of people like Paul Allen, Bill Gates and Ed Roberts himself, people who wanted their own computer.

In fact, some people were so enthusiastic that they camped outside Ed's factory while they waited for their Altairs. They were in love with the idea of personal computing.

The Altair was named after a planet from the TV show *Star Trek*. And on paper, it did sound like something from science fiction: a small, cheap computer that everyone could use in their own home. But in reality the Altair could not do very much at all. It was not much like today's personal computers (PCs). There was no keyboard, no screen and no printer. Programs were loaded bit by bit, by moving switches on the front of the machine. The results were shown by little lights that could be turned on and off. The memory was tiny. And there was no software at all. This was the perfect opportunity for Bill Gates and Paul Allen.

◆

To be useful, the Altair needed a programming language. Then users could write their own programs more easily. Bill Gates and Paul Allen told Ed Roberts that they could sell him one.

In reality, the program largely existed in Bill and Paul's head. Even after they had written the software, they did not have a chance to run it on a computer before Paul went to New Mexico.

When Paul arrived at MITS and met Ed Roberts for the first time, he was nervous:

'I hope this works . . .' he said.

'So do I,' said Ed.

In fact, Paul thought that probably the program would not work. And he became even more nervous as all of the people at MITS gathered around him. He loaded the software on to the Altair, one instruction at a time. Every mistake meant that he had to start again. Finally all of the instructions were loaded into the tiny computer's memory. Paul pressed the last switch and held his breath.

It worked! Paul could hardly believe it. The program ran, and it could do some things that no one had ever seen on an Altair before.

'You're hired. Finish the program and we'll sell it,' said Ed Roberts.

If the program had not worked, there might not be a Microsoft today. But Paul phoned Bill Gates in Harvard and told him:

'Come on down. We've got a job.'

♦

Bill came to New Mexico and he and Paul lived across the street from MITS. Their apartment became very crowded because they hired some of their school friends to help them to finish the program. They all lived together with loud music playing most of the time. It was great fun but Paul soon became worried that they would never finish the program. Bill always seemed to delay doing any work on the software.

'Don't worry,' said Bill. 'I know how to write it. I have a design in my head. I'll get it done, don't worry about it, Paul.'

But Paul was worried because he knew Bill was due to go back to Harvard soon. Bill was still a student and the university had strict rules. Then, four days before Bill had to leave, he moved to a hotel. No one saw him for the next three days. Then he returned with an enormous sheet of paper.

'Here,' said Bill to Paul, handing him the sheet.

'What's this?' Paul asked.

'It's the program.'

'The whole program?'

'Yes.'

'You've written the whole thing in three days?'

'Yes. And now I'm going back to school.'

It was one of the most amazing efforts of programming that Paul had ever seen.

The BASIC program for the Altair was an enormous success – but not in a way that made Bill Gates and Paul Allen happy. Before it went on sale, it was copied by many Altair users, who then passed it on to their friends. There was no tradition of paying for software among computer engineers. Most of them did not think it was wrong to copy a good program. But to Bill and Paul, this copying was theft.

Bill wrote a letter to a computer newspaper, complaining about the copies. The letter soon became famous and it caused a lot of anger among Altair users. It did not make many of them change their minds about copying software. But the letter did succeed in advertising the fact that Bill Gates and Paul Allen had written the best-known program for the new Altair. More work was sure to follow.

Bill soon left Harvard and Paul left his job as an engineer at Honeywell. They saw that even small computers – 'microcomputers' – would need software. So they called themselves Microsoft. Their company would one day be more powerful than IBM.

This was the beginning of a new industry. The Altair created great excitement among all the people like Ed Roberts who really wanted their own computer. But most of these people were already skilled engineers. Before computers could become truly popular, like cars or televisions, they also had to become something that anyone could use. This next step was achieved by Apple Computer.

♦

Apple Computer was the big success story of the computer industry in the 1970s. It took a product that was ugly, unfriendly and difficult to use and turned it into something that could be found beside televisions and radios in ordinary US homes. But this was never the intention of Steve Wozniak, who designed the first Apple computer. Computers were his hobby.

Just like Bill Gates and Paul Allen, Steve fell in love with computers at school. When he was thirteen, he won a science competition by building a machine that was like a computer which could add and subtract. He also spent as much time as he could with real computers. He lived in Silicon Valley, California, the home of America's best technology companies. The engineers at these firms often allowed the teenage Wozniak to use their computers after work.

Steve – usually called 'Woz' – read computer books in the way that other children watched television. Every time a new machine was announced, he asked the company for the book that described it. Often the companies gave the book to him. He spent hours in class writing programs for machines he could never even touch. He was always inventing new programming tricks – clever ways to fit more and more instructions into a few lines of a program. He liked his programs to be as small and powerful as possible.

Woz went to work for the Hewlett-Packard computer company where he was very happy for a while. He also did some work for the video-game company Atari, where his school friend, Steve Jobs, also worked. One evening, Woz was able to feed himself and a friend on free pizzas – he won them with high scores on a video game that he had designed himself!

When the Altair appeared, Woz was just as excited as Bill Gates and Paul Allen. Although the Altair was much less powerful than the computers he worked with at Hewlett-Packard, he realized that this was the way to build his own computer. Woz had always carried around designs for computers in his head. But when he saw the Altair, he realized that his own personal computer did not need to be a big, expensive machine. The Altair proved that a real computer could be made from cheap, simple parts.

Woz joined the Homebrew Computer Club. People met there to discuss the Altair and to show each other their programs and their designs for new machines. Woz made many friends at Homebrew. The atmosphere was enthusiastic and helpful. When Woz said that his bosses at Hewlett-Packard would not give him any chips, one of his friends brought a box of parts for him to the next Homebrew meeting. Woz began to design his own computer.

He took many ideas from the Homebrew club. All of the members of the club were very generous with information. Woz gradually built his computer, including all of the features that he learned about at the meetings. But the design was special. Where other people used two chips, Woz used just one. Every part of his design was as efficient as possible:

'All the time I try to do designs that use fewer parts than anyone else,' says Woz today. 'That's my puzzle. I always think, "How can I do this faster or smaller or more cleverly?" If a good answer to a problem uses six instructions, I try to do it using five or three or two. I do tricky things that aren't normal. Every problem has a better solution when you start thinking of it differently.'

In the end, Woz had a computer that was as powerful as an Altair but used fewer parts. His friend Steve Jobs was very excited about it. Jobs was not as good an engineer as Woz – almost no one was – but he was a brilliant communicator. He was always full of energy and ideas. He decided that Woz's machine was going to change the world.

Steve Jobs thought that he and Woz should start a business to sell the machine. At first Woz was not interested. The computer was a hobby, not work, to him. But Steve Jobs would not give up and eventually Woz agreed. He sold his calculator and Steve Jobs sold his Volkswagen bus. They used the money to start Apple Computer. (Jobs chose this name because he had once had a job picking apples.) The company's first factory was Steve Jobs's parents' garage.

While Woz continued to improve his design for the computer, Steve Jobs began to design a company. He saw from the start that computers could become part of ordinary life. But the company that achieved this would need to be a real company, with professional managers and financial support.

In fact, Steve Jobs was clever enough to see that he was not the right person to run a big computer firm. He had long hair and often did not wear shoes, so he was not likely to win the trust of banks and businessmen. But he persuaded experienced managers to join Apple. Soon the company – which had not actually sold anything yet – had a professional team of managers. It also succeeded in borrowing money to begin making computers.

In January 1977, Apple moved to a small building in Cupertino, California. Woz worked on his new design – called the Apple II – while Steve Jobs organized every detail of the company. Apple employed fewer than ten people, and some of them were still in school. But Jobs was so enthusiastic that everyone believed that this tiny company would change the world.

'We're going to do it!' Jobs would say. 'We're going to build the best company in the world and make the best product that has ever been made!'

People at Apple often worked all day and all night. They were designing a very different computer to the machines that were already for sale. Steve Jobs wanted to sell computers to everyone, not just engineers. So it was important that the Apple II should look friendly and be easy to use. He hired an industrial designer who produced a smooth, narrow plastic case for the machine. At a time when most computers looked like scientific instruments, the Apple II was pale brown and all of its screws were hidden.

The Apple II was introduced in April 1977 at a trade fair in California. This was a very new idea. Before the Altair, no one paid to visit a computer show. But by the time of the fair, there were many thousands of people who wanted to find out more about this new hobby.

At the trade fair, Apple Computer rented two of the best spaces, near the entrance to the hall. The company also spent money to make sure that people noticed it. Almost all the other firms at the show used paper and glue to make their signs, but Apple paid for professional designers. Big, bright plastic signs showed the six-colour apple that represented the company.

The first four Apple II computers were finished at one o'clock in the morning on the day the fair began. So many people came to the fair that it was difficult for anyone to move. But the first thing that everyone saw was Apple's shiny sign. Beneath the sign there was a clever video program running on an enormous screen.

The trade fair's success showed everyone in the computer business that something new was happening. Computers were now more than just a hobby. They could soon be big business. Many companies would take advantage of the excitement about personal computing. But Apple was the most successful. Brilliant technology and a friendly design at a price many people could afford made Apple the star of this new industry. By the end of the summer, the company was selling equipment worth more than $250,000 each month. In five years, Apple Computer was valued at a billion dollars.

There were soon hundreds of programs for the Apple II. Many of them were games or other types of software that were designed to be fun. But then, one year after the computer went on sale, a new program appeared. It was called VisiCalc. It was the world's first electronic spreadsheet. Suddenly people who worked in finance – in fact, anyone who worked with numbers or money – had a new tool.

Dan Bricklin was one of VisiCalc's inventors, and he soon found that he was being treated like a pop star.

'You've changed my life,' many people said to him. One man began to shake when Dan showed VisiCalc to him.

'That's what I do all week!' he said. 'I could do it in an hour with this program . . .'

Many people just reached into their pockets and offered Dan money as soon as they saw the software.

VisiCalc was the first serious business program for a personal computer. Soon it began to frighten the most powerful company in the computer industry: IBM.

When the Apple II had come on to the market, IBM was not worried. The Apple seemed like a toy. It did not seem to threaten the billion-dollar business of selling mainframes to the world's largest companies. This was a market that IBM understood completely. Big business wanted powerful computers that never broke down and it did not care that each machine cost a hundred thousand dollars. But VisiCalc changed that.

People who had to queue for time on an IBM mainframe were suddenly freed by VisiCalc. Why wait days for your answers when an Apple II and VisiCalc could supply them in seconds? Many business people bought an Apple computer simply because they wanted to use the new software.

This was also the time when the banking and insurance industries were changing in the USA and Britain. New laws meant that the world of finance was much more competitive. People could not afford to wait for time on an IBM mainframe. Waiting was not just annoying; it could also mean that you went out of business.

By 1979 IBM could not ignore Apple. There were suddenly tens of thousands of people buying Apples, and they were very happy with them. In fact they loved them. And they took them to the engineering departments of IBM's customers.

'I'm using my Apple because you can't do the job on the mainframe,' they said.

IBM knew that it had to do something. It was losing the hearts and minds of its customers. But it could not act quickly. It was famous for slow, careful work. It had a fixed system for designing new products. Every decision about the design was checked by many managers. Every part of a new machine was tested many times. All of the checks and tests were intended to make sure that IBM machines almost never broke down. But someone once calculated that it would take IBM nine months to produce an empty box.

Bill Lowe ran a small IBM research laboratory in Boca Raton, Florida. He knew the company was in trouble and believed he had a solution. He would change the tradition of IBM that every single part of a computer must be built by the company itself.

Bill Lowe went to his boss, Frank Carey.

'What are we going to do, Bill?' Frank Carey asked. 'Apple is hurting us. They're making us look stupid.'

'Well, I think we can build our own personal computer.'

'No,' said Frank Carey. 'At IBM it would take four years and three hundred people to do anything. That's just a fact of life.'

'No, sir,' said Bill Lowe. 'I can build an IBM personal computer in a year.'

'Tell me what you need,' said Frank Carey.

'I really need permission to go outside IBM. If I can hire outside firms to do the engineering work, I can get the job done in a year.'

'But we've never done that. It's not the IBM way.'

'I think it's the only way now, sir.'

'OK. I hope you're right. Hire whoever you want.'

IBM would soon produce the most successful computer in history. But at the same time the company would lose control of the computer industry.

The company that was Bill Lowe's first choice to write the software for the new PC missed the meeting. His second choice was the team that had written the first useful program for the Altair – Microsoft, the company started by Bill Gates and Paul Allen. Microsoft was now in Seattle, Bill and Paul's home. Bill Gates dropped all his other projects to meet the men from IBM. He even put on a suit.

IBM was hoping for an 'operating system'. The operating system is the most important software on any computer; it controls how everything else works. It usually takes an enormous amount of work to write an operating system.

Microsoft did not have an operating system. But, as before with the Altair, Bill Gates believed he could quickly create the program that was needed. IBM agreed, and Bill went away and bought an operating-system program from another Seattle software company. This program became DOS, the operating system of many millions of PCs. It was also the beginning of the flood of cash that would make Bill Gates the richest man in the world.

The deal that IBM made with Bill Gates was unusual. IBM would help Microsoft to create the operating system. It would also pay Microsoft for every single copy of the program. But Microsoft would own the program, and it could sell DOS to any company that wanted it.

Bill Lowe kept his promise: the IBM PC was created very quickly. But it was more successful than anyone imagined. The computer was first sold in 1981. IBM believed that it might sell half a million computers by 1984. In fact it sold two million.

People used to say, 'No one ever lost his job for choosing IBM.' Now these business buyers could choose an IBM PC. The IBM label meant that business trusted the machine: IBM did not make 'toys'. So the personal computer was soon accepted as a serious business tool. And as soon as business was buying these machines, their price began to fall and many more people began to buy them for use at home and at school. IBM changed from a company with thousands of customers who bought million-dollar machines to a company with millions of customers who bought thousand-dollar machines.

However, IBM soon lost control of this enormous new market. Anyone could copy the design of the PC and then buy the operating system from Microsoft. New computer companies like Compaq quickly did this. Soon they began to sell many more PCs than IBM. IBM remained a big, powerful company but it would never again have complete control of its industry.

In the 1980s, computers became common. They began to appear in every area of life. And when they were connected together, they created the Internet that we know today.

Chapter 5   The World Wide Web

The land around Geneva in the Swiss Alps is beautiful mountain countryside. People travel here from all over the world for holidays and winter sports. But among the farms and the lakes and the hotels, there are also some of the largest, most powerful and most expensive scientific tools on Earth. One of these machines is an enormous ring that spins tiny pieces of matter around in 27-kilometre circles. When they are travelling at nearly the speed of light, the machine forces them to crash together. Scientists study the resulting explosions, hoping to discover more about the building blocks of the universe.

This is the home of CERN, Europe's centre for research into high-energy physics. CERN explores what matter is made from and what holds it together. It is not the type of scientific laboratory that produces practical inventions. But there, in 1989, Tim Berners-Lee invented the World Wide Web.

◆

Tim is an English engineer with computers in his blood: both of his parents worked on the first commercial computer made in Britain, the Ferranti Mark 1. In 1980, Tim got a job at CERN for six months, and during this time he wrote a program called 'Enquire Within'.

This name comes from a popular British book that was first published in 1856. The book is full of advice and information on all sorts of different topics – from how to clean blood from a shirt to how to get married.

Tim's program aimed to organize his thoughts in the same way that the book organizes its information. He wanted to find a way to create links among a wide variety of topics that interested him. He says that brains are supposed to be good at remembering the relationships between lots of different things – but sometimes *his* brain was not very good at this. Enquire Within was the answer.

With the program, Tim could make electronic connections

within documents. He could also make connections between different documents on different computers. So, if Tim was interested in apples, he could link all of the paragraphs in a document that were about apples. And if there was a really good apple-database on another computer, he could make a link to that as well.

Enquire Within was new because it could organize information according to the content of documents, not where they could be found. It was 'hypertext'.

Ordinary text is anything that is written – a book, a letter, or a document on a computer screen. To make sense of a text, you read it from beginning to end. A hypertext is a special kind of text that is intended to give more freedom to the reader (and the writer). It contains links that lead to other places. They can lead to other texts, but also to pictures or programs or musical recordings. There is no single path through a hypertext. Readers can choose the path that suits them best.

'The power of a hypertext link is that it can link to anything,' says Tim. 'That was the central idea. You ought to be able to make a link to anything that is sitting on a computer disk anywhere. If the computer is connected to a network, you ought to be able to give it an address and link to it.'

◆

Tim says that CERN is 'a web-like place'. Scientists come to CERN from all over the world. Some stay, but many go back to their own laboratories and universities, which use many different types of computer and software. But the scientists still want to communicate and share information:

There were always different sorts of people from different countries who brought different sorts of computing equipment. So CERN was one of the first places to work on getting files from one computer system to another, getting e-mail across borders and into another system. That was the spirit. There was a lot of networking.

It was possible to get something from a distant computer at this time. But you had to be a computer expert to do it:

> It was technically simple to go and get something. But you had to be an expert of the highest degree to find your way through all the networks, to use all the programs that you found on your way, and to use the right commands to get the data back. And it was likely that, when you got something back, you would not be able to read it anyway, because it was from a different computer system.

♦

In 1989, when Tim was again working at CERN, he decided to try to make communication between the scientists easier. He believed that hypertext could help the scientists to work more efficiently because it could create paths through CERN's web.

In March 1989, Tim wrote a plan saying that a hypertext project was going to be very important for the scientists who were connected with CERN. He took the plan to his bosses:

'This is interesting,' they said. 'But it's not really our kind of project, is it? We don't do information technology here. We do high-energy physics.'

'But a hypertext system will really help CERN!' said Tim.

'Yes, well . . . thank you. We'll think about it.'

Tim saw that he was not going to persuade his bosses to build a hypertext system. But soon he had another idea. There was a coffee room between the scientists' offices and the computer rooms. So the people who needed to use the information were constantly meeting the people who ran the computers. By talking to the right people, Tim began to create support for his plan:

'Don't you get tired of translating data for the scientists?' he said to the computer people.

'Yes. There are too many computer systems around here,' they replied.

'But if there was a single program that organized all the different types of data?'

'That would be great. But there isn't, is there?'

'Not yet,' said Tim.

He spoke to the scientists as well.

'Don't you get tired of all the extra work you have to do on computers? Wouldn't you like to be able to concentrate on the physics.'

'Yes, but what can we do?'

'You need a program that allows you to make easy links between your research and everybody else's work.'

'That sounds great,' said the scientists. 'But where can we get a program like that?'

'I can write it for you,' said Tim.

♦

In October 1989, Tim started writing a program that he called 'World Wide Web'. When you were reading something interesting on the computer screen, you could just choose a phrase and link it to another document. Then you just needed to hit a 'hot key' and the other document appeared on screen. (A hot key is a key on a computer's keyboard that is programmed to do something special when it is pressed.)

At first 'World Wide Web' was the name of Tim's program. Today the World Wide Web – or simply, the 'Web' – is all of the billions of documents on millions of computers that can be read by the 'browsers' that have followed Tim's original program.

In ordinary life, if you 'browse', you look at a variety of things, hoping that some of them will be interesting. People browse through newspapers, or in bookshops or museums. If you want to, you can browse through a book, though most books are written to be read from beginning to end. But a hypertext is designed for browsing. Tim's original browser program allowed writers to create links to anything they liked, and it allowed readers to follow their interests from link to link.

The program used a new invention, a system of addresses. The system means that anything, anywhere on the Internet can have its own special address. The addresses are called 'URLs'. The Web browser understands what to do with anything that has a URL.

Tim also invented a set of rules for sending text and pictures over the Internet. The rules allow a document to appear almost exactly the same, whatever computer system is being used.

For Web authors, Tim also created a new computer language called HTML. This is the language in which all Web documents are written. It controls how text and pictures are shown on a computer screen.

◆

Together, these inventions changed the world of the Internet. The Internet of the 1980s was a place for computer experts. Since the 1990s, anyone with a computer has been able to use it. For most people, the Web browser is the friendliest program they ever use.

People at CERN began using Tim's browser in 1990. In 1991, CERN put the browser software on the Internet, so that it was free to anyone who wanted it. Within four years, the World Wide Web was the most popular use of the Net.

Tim Berners-Lee believes that the success of the Web gives hope to dreamers everywhere:

When you really believe in a dream of how things could be, then you follow the dream and it's very, very satisfying to see it work. It's exciting that you can have an idea and it can take off and it can happen. It means that dreamers all over the world should take off and not stop.

Tim's browser gave an idea to a group of young programmers in the USA. In just a few years, the business they started would take off and become the fastest-growing company that the world has ever seen – Netscape Communications.

Chapter 6   Netscape

'This software's going to change everything. Soon everyone will be using it,' Marc Andreessen said to John Doerr. John often heard claims like this. His job was finding finance for new companies. So every day he met people who were confident that their ideas were going to change the world and make millions of dollars in the process. But Marc and his plan were different.

Marc was only twenty-three years old, but already he had a good reason to be confident. A few months before, he had written a program called Mosaic. Now two million people were using it.

'I suppose you don't need to be a scientist to realize that there is a big market there,' said John Doerr. John loaned Marc the money he wanted for his business. Marc's company would soon be the fastest growing firm in history.

◆

Everything would soon change on the Internet. Tim Berners-Lee had invented the World Wide Web, which made the Internet easy to use. But it was equally important that the law of the Internet had changed.

Until 1992, John Doerr's idea of an Internet 'market' was not just ambitious; it was actually illegal. The Internet was built with US government money, and the government did not allow anyone to make a profit from it. This changed in November 1992, when President Bush signed a law that allowed commercial use of the network.

Soon there were many hundreds of new businesses on the Web. It became the most fashionable topic for the business pages of the world's newspapers. The Web was so popular – it must be the future of business. Billions of dollars would surely follow.

The problem was that, before Marc Andreessen came along, no one had found a way to make very much money from an Internet business.

◆

Two years before Marc Andreessen walked into John Doerr's office, he was not planning to change the world. He was working at a boring, low-paid job because he needed the cash.

Marc worked at the University of Illinois. There he wrote software for very large mainframe computers – enormously powerful machines that are mainly used to solve very difficult problems in science and engineering. But Marc did not find the work interesting. In fact, he was very bored.

'This kind of computing is dying!' he often said to his friend Eric Bina. 'It really should be dead already. PCs are the way forward.'

While Marc programmed the mainframes, he also spent lots of time playing on the Internet. Marc and his friends at the university all loved the new World Wide Web. But Marc also believed it could be better. There were no pictures on Web pages. And the browser still needed typed commands: it did not have the kind of interface that personal computers had made popular.

By this time, nearly all PCs drew windows, menus and buttons on their screens. These represented files, commands and processes, so the user could control the computer very easily without typing lines of strange numbers and letters.

One night, very late, Marc decided to do something about this.

'At the moment, the Web's just a tool for researchers and scientists,' he said to his friends. 'You need to be a computer programmer if you want to use it. But it could be so much better.'

'How?' his friends asked.

'The Web needs a human face. I'm going to do a browser that looks like a PC program, that works like one as well, so that anyone can use it.'

'Do we really need it? We know how the Net works.'

'But we're all programmers. The Web is full of things for programmers, but there's nothing there that a normal person would want to see.'

'What do you mean, "normal"?'

'I mean the Web should have music and art and news and . . . everything! But if there's a browser that anyone can use, if it's just like all the other software on a home computer, then we might finally get some interesting material on the Web.'

◆

Marc decided that the browser would be called 'Mosaic', and he persuaded his friend Eric Bina to join the project. They were a good team. Eric was a brilliant programmer while Marc had the ideas and drove the project forward. Marc was an unusual engineer because he had many interests outside computing. He saw how good the Mosaic browser could be because it was just the sort of program that he wanted, to find out more about music, literature and politics.

Marc and Eric worked day and night for months. Sometimes they worked for four days without a break, then slept for a day. Their attitude spread to some of their friends at the university, who joined the project to make sure that Mosaic would run on many different types of computer.

Mosaic's 'human face' for the Internet had two main features that made the program different from previous browsers. First, users did not have to type commands when they wanted to follow links, as they did in Tim Berners-Lee's browser. Instead, users of Mosaic could just point to words that were shown in a different colour or style to the rest of the text. Second, and most important, Mosaic could show pictures.

Everyone who saw the result loved it. It was like turning radio into television.

◆

Marc and Eric put Mosaic on the university's network at the start of 1993. It spread like a forest fire, and Marc quickly saw that they could make money from something that was so popular:

> The number of Mosaic users went from the original twelve to a hundred to a thousand to ten thousand to somewhere around a million by the end of 1993. So you didn't need a lot of imagination to realize that if this growth continued, it was soon going to be up to five or ten million people. That starts to be an interesting commercial opportunity.

Mosaic was creating enormous excitement among Internet users. And it was actually causing the World Wide Web itself to grow.

'People suddenly realized, "Here's the most convenient way possible to share information",' says Marc. 'In some cases it was very useful information that they needed to share anyway. In some cases it was just because they wanted to, and that still continues.'

Suddenly almost anyone with a computer could create a 'home page' – a personal document that can be seen by everyone on the World Wide Web. There are home pages about almost everything imaginable, from politics, religion and the state of the world to the author's meetings with creatures from other planets. It costs almost nothing to make a home page, and any home page can be seen by an audience of many millions.

Some people worried about this new situation, including Tim Berners-Lee. In the summer of 1993, Tim met Marc and complained about Mosaic:

'Why did you put pictures in it? That was a really bad thing.'

'What's the problem?' said Marc. 'Don't you like pictures?'

'Of course I do. But look what's happening. All the home pages and pictures of everyone's pets. It all takes up space. That isn't what the Web is for.'

'I like pictures,' said Marc. 'Lots of people like them. What's the problem? Don't be so serious about it. It's just fun.'

Marc thought that the people at CERN were mainly interested in the Web as a research project. They did not really see it as a practical tool that many other people could use for lots of different purposes. But that was why Marc had written Mosaic: to make the Web useful and fun for people who were not scientists or engineers.

◆

Marc and his friends enjoyed the success of the Mosaic browser. But they did not like what happened next.

John Mittelhauser, one of Mosaic's original programmers, came running to see Marc one day in December 1993. He was obviously angry.

'Have you seen this?' he shouted, holding the business pages of *The New York Times*.

'What is it?' Mark asked.

'It's today's *Times*. There's a big story on Mosaic.'

'That's . . . good, isn't it?'

'No, it isn't. From the story, you'd think that someone else wrote the program. Look.'

Marc read the newspaper. The story contained a big photograph of their boss at the university. It was long and enthusiastic, saying that Mosaic was 'so different and so obviously useful that it could create a new industry'. But there was no mention of Marc or of any of the other programmers who had created Mosaic without any help from the university.

'You see?' said John. 'Before Mosaic, the bosses didn't know who we were. It was just us, making plans at two o'clock in the morning over pizzas and Cokes. Now they're taking over.'

◆

John Mittelhauser was right. Their bosses at the university began to take over the project. The programmers suddenly found themselves in meetings with forty people, planning their next features. But none of the programmers thought that the bosses really understood the program or its achievements.

Marc had a theory about why the university bosses were interested in Mosaic.

'They're getting millions of dollars per year in government money for mainframe computing,' he told Eric Bina. 'And no one really wants to use mainframes any more. So they've got two choices. They can give up the government money. Or they can find something else to do. But you know that if you work at a university, you never give up government money. So you look for something else to do. They saw Mosaic and took it over.'

Marc saw that he would not be in control of Mosaic if he stayed at the university. He left Illinois and went straight to

Silicon Valley in California, the home of America's computer industry.

◆

At this time, one of Silicon Valley's most famous businessmen was looking for a new project. Jim Clark had built SGI into a company worth billions of dollars, making small, powerful computers that were designed to be linked in a network. But he no longer controlled the company he had started and he did not agree with the direction it was now taking.

Jim left SGI in January 1994. He intended to start a new company. But he did not have a clear idea of what this new firm should do.

Bill Foss was one of Jim's friends at SGI. Jim spoke to Bill on his last day at the company.

'Do you know any good engineers?' he asked. 'I want to find some good people with ideas.'

Bill had learned from the Web that Marc Andreessen was now in Silicon Valley. So he found Marc's telephone number, gave it to Jim and said, 'Give him a call. People say he's a bright engineer.'

To show Jim what Marc could do, Bill loaded Mosaic on to a computer. This was the first time Jim had seen the World Wide Web. Before he was finished, he sent an e-mail to Marc.

'You may not know me, but I started SGI.'

Jim asked Marc if he would like to meet him the next day. Of course, Marc did know who Jim Clark was and he agreed to the meeting immediately.

◆

Jim and Marc met many times in the next few weeks. Marc was shy at first, but gradually he began to argue that Jim should start an Internet company.

'We should do a "Mosaic killer",' he said. 'A new Web browser that's clearly better than Mosaic. It's the obvious thing to do.'

'I don't understand,' said Jim. 'How is it obvious?'

'Just look at how many people are using Mosaic,' said Marc. 'And look at the Web: it's taking over the Internet. The size of the Net is doubling every year and a half, so by the time we get some products on the market, fifty million people will be on the Net. You've got to be able to make money with fifty million people using your product. We have to get into this business.'

'But every person I talk to tells me, "No one makes money on the Net." I'm supposed to be in business!'

'That doesn't make any sense!' said Marc. 'It's just like saying, "Who's going to sell the first telephone? Who's going to buy it? Who will they call?" Someone always has to be first. In every new market there's a company that takes a risk and gets very rich.'

Jim listened to Marc and eventually he said, 'I'll put money into that. Personally I don't know how we'll make money, but I'll put money into it and we'll find a way to make money later. There's got to be a way to make a profit in a market that's growing as quickly as this.'

♦

Jim and Marc flew out to the University of Illinois to see Marc's friends who had helped to write Mosaic. Jim would only start the new company if he could hire all of the original team of engineers. This was not difficult because, as Eric Bina says, life was 'sad and much quieter' since the university had taken over and Marc had left.

So Marc's friends came to Silicon Valley and Mosaic Communications was born – and quickly died. The name 'Mosaic' and all of the software were owned by the University of Illinois, not by the people who had created the program.

'I didn't think they'd care,' said Jim. 'In fact, I thought they'd be pleased. Other universities like to see their graduates start businesses.'

'They didn't like us very much, in the end,' said the programmers.

'Yes, they're probably upset that I've stolen you all away when you were working like slaves for them.'

In April 1994, the company became Netscape Communications and Jim made sure that the new software did not contain any of the Mosaic program.

◆

The engineers had to write a new browser and a new Web 'server' (the program that sits on a distant computer and delivers Web pages to browsers). Both programs had to be faster than Mosaic, with more features. They also had to crash less often than Mosaic.

When a program crashes, it freezes so that it cannot be used any more. Sometimes the computer must be switched off and on again. Mosaic crashed all the time, and Jim Clark was not pleased.

'This is terrible. I can't sell something like this. Would you buy a car that drove off the road every half an hour?'

'Don't worry,' said John Mittelhauser, trying to calm Jim. 'We were students when we wrote it. We were just having fun. We weren't thinking about quality.'

'Well, think about quality now!' said Jim.

The engineers began to work. For a time, they seemed to do nothing except work:

'People are often there for forty-eight hours without a break, just writing software,' Bill Foss said to Jim Clark. Bill had just been hired at Netscape and he was amazed by the atmosphere at the company. 'I've never seen anything like it.'

Marc Andreessen's positive attitude was a big force driving the work. He walked around saying, 'I have a dream! I have a dream! We will succeed in the end. We are fighting a war and we will win!'

◆

But Marc was not the world's best manager. Jim Clark spoke to him:

'Marc, you know you're the heart and soul of this project. You work more hours than anybody else. You're great at thinking of new ideas. You're very good at knowing what's important. You can take forty different pieces of information and put them together . . .'

'Thanks,' said Marc.

'. . . but these are very different skills from managing engineers. You're not a good manager.'

'That's not true,' said Marc. 'I am actually a terrible manager.'

'Then would it be OK with you if I hired some professional managers, so you can concentrate on what you're good at?'

'Please. That would make me very happy,' said Marc.

But he continued to work harder than anyone else at Netscape. He enjoyed the work more than anything else. His office – where he often slept – was a mess, full of every book in the world that he believed could help with this project.

Many of the books were about Bill Gates: the world's richest man, in control of the world's most successful company. All of Bill Gates's power was built on Microsoft's control of the operating system for IBM personal computers. Marc wanted to know how to be a great businessman and he felt he could learn from Gates. He thought that the main lesson was that, at first, it is more important to persuade people to use your products than to make money from them. Microsoft only began to charge high prices and make enormous profits after the IBM PC had taken over the personal computer market. So Marc decided that Netscape's browser would be free to non-commercial users. Only businesses would have to pay for it.

'We have to persuade everybody to use the browser,' Marc said to Jim. 'That's the way to give the company a fast start. It's a Microsoft lesson, right? If everyone uses your product, you've got a lot of possibilities, a lot of ways to make money from that. Market share now equals income later, and if you don't have the market share now you're not going to get the income later. Whoever gets the market share wins.'

Marc believed that the Web would be like the market for PC software: 'In a market like this there has to be just one single big winner.' Marc wanted Netscape to be the winner on the World Wide Web.

◆

On 13 October 1994, the new software was put on the Web. The engineers stayed up all night with beer and pizza to watch as the downloading began. ('Downloading' is making copies of files from the Internet.) Within an hour, their computer had crashed because demand for the software was so great.

In a few weeks, almost everyone on the World Wide Web was using Netscape's software. The browser, called Navigator, was much faster than its competitors. It could also show more interesting pages because it added new features to the HTML language.

Soon, many Web pages contained notices that said, 'This page is best viewed with Netscape Navigator'. This was free advertising and it caused millions more people to download Netscape software.

In 1993, the World Wide Web was only the eleventh largest cause of traffic on the Net. By the summer of 1995, it was number one, mainly because there were more than ten million

Netscape users. (There were still even more individual e-mail messages. But Web pages are larger computer files than most e-mail messages, so the Web caused more traffic.)

◆

Some of the first users of Netscape's products were businesses. At this time, most firms did not actually try to sell anything over the Web. But a company 'Web site' (a set of linked pages) did offer immediate advantages.

First, it could cut costs. It is much cheaper to put company information on the Web than to pay people to answer phones. Second, it could attract new business. Many people prefer to look up prices and other information on the Web than to travel to a shop or make a telephone call. Third, the Web became very fashionable, very quickly, among businesses as well as individuals.

Netscape charged businesses between $1,500 and $5,000 for the software to run a Web site. That was how the company made a profit. It made $75 million in the first year and $375 million in the second year.

On 9 August 1995, Netscape 'went public': for the first time, people could buy shares in the company. On the evening before the sale, the shares were priced at $28 each. When the market opened, they sold for more than $70. This made it the most successful sale of all time. America's main financial newspaper said, 'It took many of today's most successful companies fifty years to become corporations worth $2.7 billion. It took Netscape about a minute.'

Chapter 7   Yahoo! – A Guide to Everything

The World Wide Web contains millions of pages and it is growing more quickly every day. It is likely that hundreds of new pages will be added while you are reading this chapter. No one can say exactly how big the Web is at any moment, but it is probably bigger today than any library on Earth. Almost anything you could want to know is on the Web – somewhere. But that's the problem.

Information is no use unless you can find it. And as the Web grows, it becomes more and more difficult to find exactly what you want. One obvious answer is to let a computer do the work. There are lots of 'search engines' that use powerful computers and clever software to hunt on the Web. You give them a topic and they give you a list of the sites that seem to talk about it. But very often the list is still too long to be useful. If you want to know more about the actress Pamela Anderson, the AltaVista search engine will quickly find more than 150,000 pages for you.

More importantly, the software does not understand what it is looking for. To a computer, the word 'football' does not mean anything. It is just a string of letters. A computer does not know that American football is completely different from the game played in the rest of the world.

Yahoo! is one of the most popular sites on the Web – with millions of visitors every day – because it uses a different way of searching the Internet. Instead of computers, Yahoo! employs people to 'surf' the Web. Yahoo!'s professional surfers spend all day looking at Web sites. If they think a site is good, interesting or important, they add it to Yahoo!'s guide to the Web. The principle behind the system is that any site can be fitted into one of fourteen categories.

When you go to Yahoo!, you see these fourteen categories first. Some of the categories are Arts, Business, Computers & Internet, Education, Entertainment, Government, News, Sports, Science, and Society & Culture. It is always fun to try to think of a topic or a Web page that could not be put into one of Yahoo!'s categories. But it is hard to succeed at this game. The categories have been tested over many years. And anyway, the fourteen categories are only the surface of Yahoo! Each of them contains many other, smaller categories which each contain even smaller categories. Some of the topics in the smallest categories are so odd that you cannot believe anyone in the world knows anything about them. Just the page's author, perhaps?

Yahoo! is clever because it is so well organized. Many other sites have copied the idea of breaking the Web into categories but none of them is as well organized as Yahoo! In a world of new technology, Yahoo!'s strength is human intelligence.

◆

Yahoo!'s creators, Jerry Yang and Dave Filo, met at Stanford University. They were both graduate students who stayed at the university because they did not feel ready for jobs. Today Jerry says, 'I wasn't really ready to work. I had a good degree but I didn't have the experience and I wasn't grown-up enough for it. I wasn't even twenty-one. So I looked for ways to stay in school.' Dave Filo felt the same way. Dave was a little older than Jerry and in fact he had once been Jerry's teacher – 'He gave me a B!' complains Jerry, who was used to getting As. But they also worked together, and Jerry gratefully remembers that Dave did all the work: 'He wrote the whole program. I didn't do anything. So I knew then that I was going to have to work with him more often.'

They did spend more and more time together. They were – and still are – a great team. Dave is a brilliant engineer, Jerry is a brilliant talker. Dave is messy, Jerry is neat. When one can't do something, the other probably can. But Jerry says that Yahoo! started because he always felt 'about half a step behind' Dave on the Internet:

'Dave always had this talent for finding things. I was always trying to find out how he knew everything.'

Dave and Jerry had a tiny office in a university hut at Stanford. Both of them were still doing university work. They wanted to go into business but did not know what to do. Then Dave discovered Mosaic.

Both of them quickly became Web experts. They spent hours on the Internet and their university work began to suffer. But this was when Yahoo! really started. Dave and Jerry both began to make lists of their favourite Web sites. They showed their new discoveries to each other all the time and eventually joined their lists together. The result was *Jerry's Guide to the World Wide Web*.

But soon things got out of control. There were so many sites that Dave and Jerry had to organize the list. They broke it into categories, and when the categories became too big, they broke them into smaller categories. This is still the way Yahoo! works today.

It was quickly obvious that lots of people outside the hut also wanted a guide to the Web. Soon hundreds of people were viewing *Jerry's Guide* every day. This came as a surprise to Dave and Jerry. They had never thought about an audience. But the guide was a Web site like any other site. It was on Stanford's network, which was on the Internet. So anyone with a connection to the Internet could look at the guide.

This sudden audience was not just looking at the guide. It was also suggesting ways to improve it. People started sending in their own favourite Web addresses. If Dave and Jerry liked them, they included these sites in the guide. Then they began to ask people to suggest good Web sites. The result was a flood of e-mail. Both Jerry and Dave found that they loved this attention. And it was often very helpful: they were able to make the guide better, which led to more traffic, more e-mails, more sites in the guide.

After a few weeks, Jerry decided to change the name of the site to *David and Jerry's Guide to the World Wide Web*.

'Why are you changing it?' said Dave. 'I don't want my name on it.'

'I know,' said Jerry. 'That's why I did it. Now you'll have to think of a better name.'

At first Dave only knew that the name had to start with Y–A. Lots of his favourite computer programs were 'Ya–something', because the authors were often too exhausted to invent an original name by the time they had finished the program. So they just called it 'Yet Another' news-reader, or 'Yet Another' e-mail program.

Dave and Jerry sat down with a dictionary.

'Ya–'

'Yataghan!'

'Yataghan??'

'Yes. "A type of Turkish short sword with a double curved blade".'

'How about "Yankee"?'

'Or "Yang"?'

'Very funny.'

Eventually they decided on 'Yahoo!' They just liked the sound of it.

By the winter of 1994, the traffic was so heavy that Dave remembers that he was 'hoping it wouldn't grow so quickly'. There was not much time to eat or sleep. But this was also the time that Netscape went public. The world was suddenly mad about the Web. Dave and Jerry began to think that there must be a way to turn all this traffic into a business. Surely it must be worth something.

They thought seriously about selling. A big Internet company called AOL was interested in buying Yahoo! It was the world's largest commercial Internet service and it wanted a search engine. AOL made Dave and Jerry an offer that would make them very rich, very quickly. The company also warned them that if they did not sell, they would soon be competing with AOL itself.

Dave and Jerry thought hard about the offer.

'What do you think?' Jerry asked.

'It's a nice idea,' said Dave. 'It would be nice to be rich.'

'Yes. And I don't much like the idea of competing with AOL.'

'No. But if we take the money, we'll have to work there. For years.'

'With the suits and the office politics . . .'

'Not much fun there.'

'It wouldn't be *David and Jerry's Guide*, would it?'

'No. And they'd kill "Yahoo!" when they'd worked out how to run it – it'd become "AOL Search" or something.'

'But can we really do it ourselves? Start a business?'

'Let's find out.'

So Dave and Jerry decided to stay in control of Yahoo! In April 1995, they borrowed $4 million to turn Yahoo! into a proper business.

◆

Netscape had also been interested in buying Yahoo! They offered a similar deal to AOL's. They needed a search engine for their Web browser. Dave and Jerry had refused Netscape's offer as well. For a time they worried that they would soon be competing with two big rivals – AOL and Netscape.

However, in the end Netscape gave Yahoo! an enormous amount of free business. Netscape did not create its own search engine; it simply put a link to Yahoo! in its Web browser. This meant that Yahoo! was suddenly the obvious first step for many millions of Web searches.

Dave and Jerry used the $4 million to turn Yahoo! into a

proper company. They began to hire managers and professional surfers. The surfers meant that, for the first time, Dave and Jerry did not have to look at every new site themselves.

One of the new managers was Tim Koogle, who was hired by Dave and Jerry to be the chief manager. Like them, he came from Stanford's engineering department. His job was to decide how to make money from this amazingly popular – but free – service.

Advertising was the obvious answer to this problem. Yahoo! began to sell space on its pages in August 1995. It was no surprise when the change was greeted by a flood of angry e-mail from existing users:

'I can't believe you're doing this!'

'We thought Yahoo! was different, but now it's just like any other business.'

But the e-mail soon stopped. And if the people who wrote it did stop using Yahoo! when the advertising appeared, Yahoo! did not notice. There was never any fall in traffic at the site.

Yahoo! also introduced some other changes in the summer of 1995. Perhaps the most important of these was a news service. Yahoo! made a deal with Reuters, one of the world's largest news organizations. Reuters supplied news that could be viewed directly on Yahoo!'s pages. This was Yahoo!'s first step to becoming a destination as well as a guide that sent people to other sites.

Soon other services were added, including weather, share prices and travel news. Yahoo! was becoming like an electronic newspaper or a computerized television channel: the first place to look for information, news or fun.

By February 1996, Yahoo! was serving six million pages a day. Eighty companies were paying for advertising on the site.

Yahoo! went public in March 1996, and its shares were valued at $850 million. Dave and Jerry were amazed. Yahoo!'s value was two hundred times greater than it had been just a year earlier.

They had known for some time that they would soon be rich. But they had never imagined that they would be worth so much. Their small company was now more valuable than some of America's largest airlines, car firms and banks. It was a sign that the US public expected great things of the Internet. Dave and Jerry realized that they had started the twenty-first century four years before the rest of the world.

Chapter 8 The Future

It is impossible to say what the Internet will be like in the future, or how it will change our lives. Just ten years ago, very few people had heard of it. Now it is nearly as common and useful as the telephone. As more and more people use the Internet, as it becomes cheaper and faster and easier to use, there will be new things on the Internet that we cannot imagine today. But perhaps some of the more surprising things that have happened recently can give us a taste of the future.

Anyone can report on the world

Using just a cheap PC, Matt Drudge nearly ended the career of US president Bill Clinton. Many other journalists at big news organizations knew about the possibility of a sexual relationship between Clinton and Monica Lewinsky. They chose not to report it. Matt Drudge did not work for anyone, but he wrote the story and put it on the Internet. Soon a million people a day were looking at his Web site.

Matt Drudge believes that traditional journalists are too friendly with the people they write about. Now, with the Internet, the future belongs to ordinary people with a story to tell.

Internet crime

Vladimir Levin worked for a computer firm in St Petersburg, Russia. From there, using the Internet, he was able to break into Citibank's computers in the USA. He moved more than $10 million to other banks all over the world.

Most of the world's money is now stored in computers. Clever criminals are likely to use computers and the Internet, not guns, to steal it.

Free software

Today, most operating systems are the work of hundreds of programmers and they can cost thousands of dollars. In 1991, Linus Torvalds wrote an operating system alone and he gave it away. Now, with the help of many other programmers who work together on the Internet, his Linux system has grown into a serious rival to the products of the industry leader, Microsoft.

It costs almost nothing to deliver software over the Internet. If programmers are willing to give their work away, and if the programs are as good as their commercial rivals, the days of paying for software could soon be over.

Computer wars

India and Pakistan have twice fought wars over Kashmir. In 1999, the battle took a new form when the Indian army's Web site was taken over. The content of the site was removed and stories of crimes by the army against ordinary Kashmiris were put there instead.

As the Internet becomes increasingly important to governments, it also becomes a stage for people who oppose them. The information wars of the future may be fought on Web sites.

Sex

In 1995, *Time* magazine's cover showed a young child looking at sex pictures on the Internet. The story said that 83 per cent of the 'news' part of the Internet was being used to exchange sex pictures.

In fact this was not true. And there are many ways for parents to prevent their children from seeing anything on the Internet that the parents do not like. But it is true that, like photography, cinema and video before it, the Internet is growing partly because it is a way for people to find sexual material that they cannot easily obtain in any other way.

Go to work on the Internet

In Bangalore, India, thousands of computer programmers work while their US bosses are asleep. At the end of the day in Cologne, Germany, engineers send the designs of new cars to their colleagues in Dearborn, USA, who continue the work.

In the future, the place where you live may become less important than who you are and what you can do.

Are we alone in the universe?

The project SETI searches for radio messages sent by intelligent life on other planets. It looks at radio waves from every part of the sky, searching for a pattern that means that another form of life is broadcasting. The problem is that there are many hundreds of millions of possible messages, and many fewer mainframes to examine them. David Anderson of Berkeley University has an answer. His project, called SETI@Home, sends data to tens of thousands of home computers over the Internet. A program works in the background, when your computer is not doing anything else, and looks for a message in the data. So, the first contact with creatures from other worlds could happen on your PC.

ACTIVITIES

Introduction and Chapter 1

Before you read

1 When do you think that the Internet started? What was your first experience of it?

2 Find these words in your dictionary. They are all in this book. Match each word with a definition below.

armed forces republic satellite software technology

   a the use of science or knowledge in industry
   b a country with a president and a government representing the people
   c a machine in space that moves around the Earth
   d the programs which control the operation of a computer
   e the army, navy and air force of a country

After you read

3 'The Russians are in space!'
   a Why did this worry the USA?
   b What did the US president do as a result?

Chapters 2–3

Before you read

4 What do you understand by the phrase 'computer network'? What do you think is the difference between an ordinary computer network and the Internet?

5 Translate these sentences into your language. Find the words in *italics* in your dictionary.
   a My computer has *crashed* again!
   b Switch it off, and *log on* again.
   c I think it's a problem with the *hardware*.
   d I've *run* a repair program, but it hasn't helped.
   e Pass me the *keyboard*, and I'll have a look.

69

f Does your university still have a *mainframe* computer?

g I don't know; the computer department is on a different *site*.

h Software provides the *interface* between the user and the machine.

6 Find these words in your dictionary. Use them in the phrases below.

digital   distant   inner   institute   research   security

a ..... London

b ..... student

c ..... planet

d ..... guard

e ..... of education

f ..... computer

After you read

7 Answer these questions.

a What did Bob Taylor do before he worked for ARPA?

b Why wasn't he happy with ARPA's computer systems?

c How much money did he have to build the ARPAnet?

d Why was Larry Roberts happy with the ARPAnet?

e What were some of the surprise results of the network?

f Why did Bob Kahn and Vint Cerf want to build the Internet?

Chapters 4–5

Before you read

8 When was the first time that you used a personal computer? What did you use it for?

9 Find these words in your dictionary. Match them to the phrases below.

browse   chip   hypertext   matter   spreadsheet   text   web

a an important electronic part of a computer

b a network

c a program used by accountants

d to look for something

e writing

f a program that links many different texts together

g the material that everything in the universe is made of

10 Who are these people? Why were they so important to the development of personal computers?

    a Ed Roberts

    b Bill Gates and Paul Allen

    c Steve Wozniak

    d the Homebrew Computer Club

    e Dan Bricklin

    f Bill Lowe

11 Discuss the importance of Tim Berners-Lee's hypertext system to the development of the World Wide Web.

Chapters 6–8

Before you read

12 What do you think are the main reasons for the success of the World Wide Web?

13 Discuss the possible meanings of the phrases below. Then check the words in *italics* in your dictionary.

    a to divide topics into different *categories*

    b to *download* information from the Web

    c to *surf* the Web

    d to *take over* a company

After you read

14 What effect did these have on the use of the Internet?

    a a decision by President Bush

    b Mosaic

    c Netscape Navigator

    d Yahoo!

15 The book lists recent developments in the use of the Internet. What are they? Can you add others? How do you think the Internet will change in the future?

Writing

16 Write a letter to a friend who does not use the Internet. Describe how it works. Tell them why they should start using it.

17 Imagine that you are working for the US government at the time of the Cold War. Write a report explaining why the government should spend money on computer technology.

18 In your own words, write the story of how either Apple or Microsoft began.

19 Write a report for a magazine. Explain the part that Marc Andreessen played in the story of the Internet.

20 Write a letter to Yahoo! Tell them what you think of their service. Make at least one suggestion for improving it.

21 Write an e-mail to the person that you think you will be twenty years from now. Describe how you think that the Internet will change your life.